First published in the UK in 2022 by Studio Press,
an imprint of Bonnier Books UK,
4th Floor, Victoria House, Bloomsbury Square, London WC1B 4DA
Owned by Bonnier Books,
Sveavägen 56, Stockholm, Sweden

bonnierbooks.co.uk

Copyright © 2022 Disney Enterprises, Inc. All rights reserved.

All rights reserved. No part of this publication may be
reproduced or transmitted in any form or by any means,
electronic, or mechanical, including photocopying, recording,
or by any information storage and retrieval system,
without permission in writing from the publisher.

Printed in Poland
2 4 6 8 10 9 7 5 3 1

All rights reserved
ISBN 978-1-80078-403-1

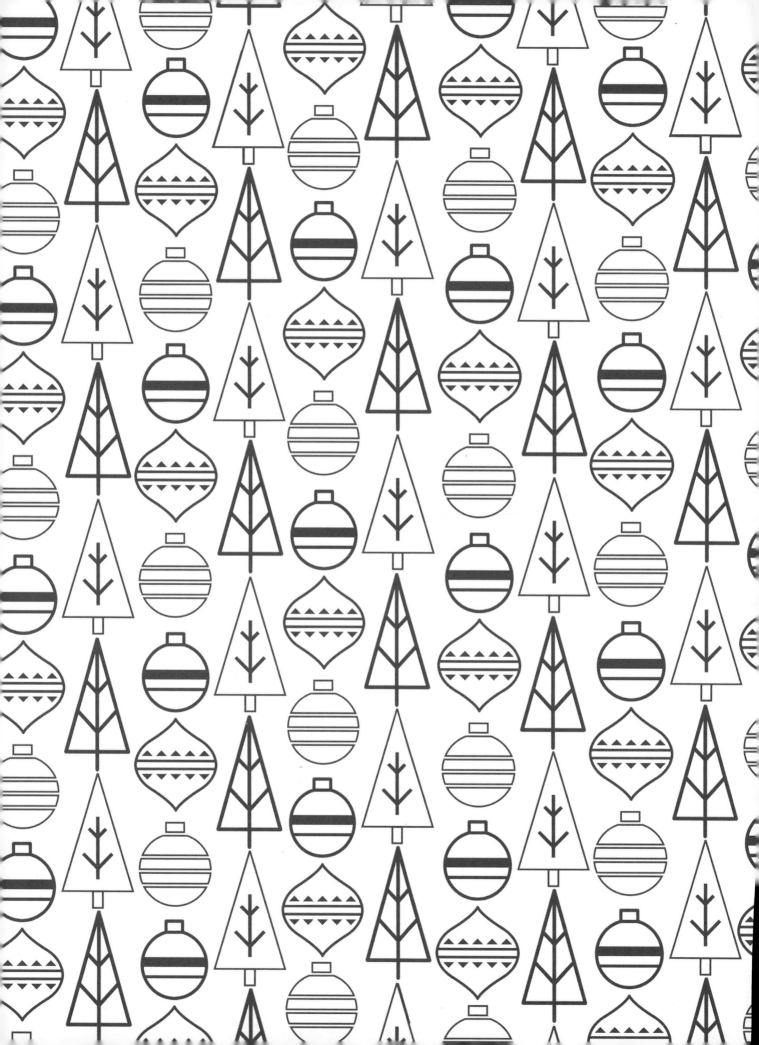